Church of Love

Third Edition

Ronda Chervin

En Route Books and Media, LLC
Saint Louis, MO

Make the time

En Route Books and Media, LLC
5705 Rhodes Avenue, St. Louis, MO 63109

Contact us at **contactus@enroutebooksandmedia.com**

Cover Credit: Sebastian Mahfood using an image of a pelican from a tabernacle in St. George Church, Antwerp, Belgium.

Copyright 1973, 1983, 2026: Ronda Chervin

ISBN-13: 979-8-88870-489-9
Library of Congress Control Number:
Available at https://catalog.loc.gov

First edition published by Liguori Publications, 1973. Second edition published by Chiaro-Oscuro, 1983. Third edition published by En Route Books and Media, LLC, 2026.

Nihil Obstat: Monsignor Robert E. Brennan, Los Angeles, California, July 12, 1972; Imprimatur: Los Angeles, September 7, 1972, John J. Ward, Vicar General of Los Angeles

All rights reserved. No part of this book may be reproduced, stored in a retrieval system, or transmitted in any form, or by any means, electronic, mechanical, photocopying, or otherwise, without the prior written permission of the author.

Table of Contents

Introduction 1

God Loves Us He Gives Himself to Us 5

God's Love is Intimate: His Sacraments are Loving

    Embraces 13

    Baptism 14

    Holy Communion... 17

    Confirmation... 23

    Penance 27

    Marriage.. 35

    Holy Orders 44

    The Anointing of the Sick 52

God's Love Transforms: His Love Makes Us True

    Christians.. 57

    Dogma... 58

    Prayer 62

Law of Love 70

The Mass 78

Love of Neighbor 84

Sanctity 88

Conclusion 101

Introduction

That God is love is the firm belief of many people. In a vague general way, they affirm this, yet they do not expect him to manifest his love in any dynamic or intimate way. They seem to have no great desire to want to know him more, to speak to him often, or to make him a real part of their life experience. Imagine a young man who thinks he loves a girl but rarely visits her—rarely speaks to her or even about her.

Such a mixture of affirmation and negation also often underlies these questions: "I do believe in God, but why do I have to believe that Christ was God?" "Why must I go to services in a building called a church? Can't I just talk to God when I feel like it and live my own life, trying to be as good as possible?"

The religious person probably can present learned reasons for belief in Christ and the Church. Or, if one has despaired of communication through reasoning, one may just shrug one's shoulders and say, "It comes down to faith: I have it and you don't!"

Questions involving doubt about Christ and the Church are very much related to questions about love. Therefore, one of the best approaches to them is to delve into the nature of love and to show that many aspects of Catholicism (as well as other religions), which a person may think are unnecessary encumbrances or even distortions, really follow directly from the one truth that "God is love." (Jn. 4:8)

So, what I shall say in this little book is to examine the main aspects of Catholic faith and life to show the way in which such elements as prayer, faith, dogma and the sacraments are manifestations of God's love. This shall be done by means of constant comparisons with the way a human lover acts and thinks. As the great French thinker Pascal wrote so many centuries ago, "The heart has its reason ..." and there is a logic to love which is as compelling as the proofs of formal syllogisms.

There are many, many ways of defining love. Each of us probably has our own way of thinking of it. But there are certain ingredients in love which everyone would agree on. Three of these, which I shall make the basis of this study, are <u>love as self-giving</u>, as <u>intimate</u>, and as <u>transforming</u>.

Church of Love was first printed in 1972. Since then, there have been quite a few changes in the Church. The revised edition reflects new ways of administering the sacraments as well as the emphasis on Scripture.

The <u>Afterword</u> of the original edition with its brief story of my conversion proved to be so intriguing to many readers that I have expanded it as a separate book under the title *The Search for the Saviour* (published by Chiaro-Oscuro).

God Loves Us

He Gives Himself to Us

Everyone who loves wants to give. A young man may give his girlfriend many presents. But if he gave her everything she could want, and kept him<u>self</u> withdrawn, she would become unhappy.

Understanding and good advice are another form of giving. But they can never be the same as <u>self</u>-giving. Think how a man feels when the girl he loves cannot reciprocate in kind but instead offers to be his friend, available to help him with his problems.

All this is obvious enough to those who have experienced love. Yet, many people think that "God is love" can be understood without reference to <u>self</u>-giving. They will say or think "God expressed his love for us by giving us the gift of life. He set us on the road, and now it is up to us to find our way in purely human terms." Others say, "What difference does it make whether Christ was divine or not? What counts is that he gave us his wonderful teachings about how to live and love."

I believe that God expresses his love continually through <u>self</u>-giving, and that this truth is exemplified most vividly in the fact that Christ is divine. Christ is God's gift of him<u>self</u> to us.

> 'Lord,' Philip said to him, 'show us the Father and that will be enough for us.' 'Philip,' Jesus replied, 'after I have been with you all this time, you still do not know me? Whoever has seen me has seen the Father ... Do you not believe that I am in the Father and the Father is in me?' (Jn 14:8-10)

If Christ were but a wise teacher, or even the greatest sage of all time, still he could go no further than to offer his disciples the truth. Only if Christ is divine can he come into each person's self to make his teaching begin from within, not merely as new thoughts but as new life.

Christ gives himself to his people gradually. He knows that they have the rebellious divided spirit of adolescents—full of longing for genuine love, yet plagued with disappointment, despair, and doubt. He treats them somewhat like an older and experienced man might win the confidence of a wild young girl. Slowly, Christ gathers them to himself by the magnetic attraction of his grace. He wins them by deeds of love, healing them of their miseries, curing their leprosy, exorcising their demons. Only when he sees they are ready does he begin to reveal more intimate mysteries of his love, such as his desire to become one body with his followers and the eventual unity they will achieve with him in eternity.

He knows that many of their ways are unloving, but instead of reproaching them directly, he begins by telling them parables, letting them discover for themselves how far short their own lives are from the new ideal.

Gradually, his disciples. begin to respond to Christ's self-giving. Peter, at first in awe at his Master's miracles, says, "Lord, depart from me for I am a sinful man." (Luke 5:8) Later, he replies to Christ's direct entreaty of love with the words, "Lord, you know that I love you." (John 21:17)

Once he has won their hearts, he is yet aware of the fact that they are still children and unable to grasp the full meaning of his love. Patiently, he repeats his love for them. When they betray him, he recalls them not by arguments but by a burning glance of love—the final proof being those unforgettable words, "Father, forgive them; they do not know what they are doing." (Luke 23:34) In the Resurrection, we see the triumph of his love over all those forces that are death to love. He returns to his disciples to assure them of this, and then ascends into eternity, there to love them and us forever.

The whole life of Christ proves that God wants to give himself entirely to us, even to the point of identification with all our sufferings. How deeply consoling this thought is! Otherwise, when we suffer, we are tempted to think that God sits far away in his blissful eternity indifferent to us. It seems strange that a God who is perfect can suffer. But it would be even stranger, once we understand God is love, if he could not suffer! God's love cannot be conceived as "frozen glory," which is the way many think of it.

No symbol in the history of mankind so helps us to trust in God's love in the midst of suffering as that of the Cross. There is all the difference in the world between believing that Christ was a wise human teacher, who showed us how to trust God in the midst of suffering by his own resignation to the Cross, and believing that Christ is God himself, who identifies with and participates in our suffering.

That the self-giving love of God in Christ is not to end with Christ's return to the Father is made clear in the New Testament. It is not as if one hungry for love today would have to be satisfied with reading about how God loved men in the past. He said, "Blessed are those who have not seen and yet believe." "I shall be with you for all times." "I shall not leave you." Anyone who has loved intensely knows that it is possible at times to experience the very spirit of an absent lover so profoundly that it seems that he is closer than when he was physically present. It is somewhat like the "aura" of a person that pervades the room he has just left. The feeling of his personality transcends the physical. It is perhaps for this reason that many people discover the realm of the spirit for the first time when they fall in love in a way which transcends mere physical attraction. They are participating in the spiritual reality of the beloved, even if the word "spirit" has never been part of their vocabulary.

To make the idea of the Holy Spirit more concrete to us, we should remember that he is the Spirit of love. He is the divine Love sent to infuse us with the sense of God when we read the Gospels, when we pray, when we receive the sacraments, or when we show love for other people.

It is said that the Church was born on Pentecost. On that day, the Spirit which came in the form of tongues of fire, being the Spirit of love, joined the apostles together into a united and holy group. (Acts 2) It is not possible to understand what the Church is outside of the mystery of the Spirit, that is, God's self-giving. Otherwise, it tends to be defined in purely external ways, in terms of buildings, or as a stabilizer of the morals of society, or as a purely historical entity. To think of it in such ways is as lifeless as it would be to understand marriage as simply a way society has to perpetuate and organize itself, or as a moral way of dealing with sexual urges, or merely as people living together in a certain house. Sometimes, children who cannot yet understand the mysteries of marital love do think of marriage in this external way. By analogy, a person who has not fallen in love with God who gives himself in the Church cannot understand the life of the Church; he therefore tends to judge it according to norms which disregard its inner life.

Hence, we find that one outside the inner sanctum of love in the Church may proclaim: "Unless you can show me that Catholics are better morally than anyone else—contributing more to society—why should I consider the Church to be even Christian?" Such a critic is usually nonplussed to find that although the ardent Catholic cannot prove his moral superiority, yet he feels no desire to abandon the Church. For him, the Church is the place where he experiences God's self-giving love. This is like asking someone who has just fallen in love, "What social utility does all this passionate joy have? Has it helped you to become a reformer of men?" Doubtless, the lover, as the Catholic, would hope that being in love would ultimately make him a better person; and he would realize that his questioner did not understand that the experience of love was something so great in itself that it did not need to be justified by anything else. Good should flow from all genuine love, but love, in itself, is the highest good. Just as the lover does not visit his beloved as an impetus to further good deeds, so neither does the Catholic go to Mass solely in order to do a better job of being good for the rest of the day. Yet, paradoxically, as we shall see, it is true that the more deeply a person opens himself to love for its own sake, the more likely it will be that he will be happier and less egotistic, and that ultimately he will be a vessel overflowing with love of neighbor.

God's Love is Intimate

His Sacraments are Loving Embraces

Love is never static. The lover does not simply give himself and rest. Instead, love tends toward greater and greater intimacy of union. As the human lover strives always toward getting closer and closer to the one he loves, so the divine Lover seeks means of entering deeply within us. The sacraments, often called inventions of love, are ways in which Christ concretely and visibly, yet mysteriously and intimately, enters into union with us. In this chapter, we will examine the different ways in which the various sacraments may be conceived in this light.

Before discussing each sacrament, it may be remarked that the definition of a sacrament in general as a visible sign of invisible grace is very felicitously explained by the analogy to human love. Although the essence of love itself is something invisible, ineffable, and greater than any expression of it, yet it continually seeks to become manifest in a visible form—in gifts, smiles, kisses, and embraces. Those who view God as so transcendent that it would be inconsistent for him to manifest his love in any concrete way seem to misunderstand the nature of love. The motives of such people may be to counter-balance superstition, idolatry, and exaggerated anthropomorphism; but the net effect of this tendency to emphasize transcendence is to render God impotent to express love to his creatures, and even to make it inexplicable that he should have reached out to create them at all. Often, contrary to the wishes of the original theologians who stress transcendence, the practical result of their thinking is that God is "kicked upstairs" so that "he can mind his own business," and we can proceed merrily with the destruction of the universe.

Baptism

> "Go therefore and make disciples of all nations, baptizing them in the name of the Father, and the Son and of the Holy Spirit" (Matthew 28:19)

Many say that Baptism should no longer be administered to the newborn, but only to people old enough to experience it as a free conscious act. It would take a long theological discourse to explain all the reasons why baptism is given to the infant. Here I will only discuss this in relationship to the way baptism is an expression of God's desire for intimacy with his creatures.

Although every creature is born out of the loving hand of God, yet, because of original sin, he has lost spiritual participation in God's life. He is turned toward the pursuit of worldliness rather than toward God. But Christ's redemption has removed the barrier between man and God and opened a way through him to an essential reunion. We believe that Christ embraces the spirit of his creature in baptism and seals it in a bond of love which can never be destroyed from his side, but only from ours.

Thus, the purpose of baptism is not to provide the person with a conscious religious experience, but rather to open within him a door through which divine love can flow, to turn the soul toward God by implanting on it his first kiss, as it were. To deny the child this expression of Christ's self-giving, on the grounds that the infant is too young to freely choose, would be similar to withholding parental love until the child is at the age of reason. In fact, psychological studies show that tiny orphans have actually died when they were tended impersonally, so deeply did this lack of love affect them! Given the infinite gulf between the reality of divine love and even the adult's ability to appreciate it, who shall set a time when the entering of Christ's love into the soul would have its greatest efficacy? By comparison with the love on God's part, we are always half asleep. Just as Christ has infinite love for this fresh individual uniquely conceived, so the Church, manifesting the divine love, rushes to bring the infant into contact with it by making him a member of the Mystical body of the Church.

Unless a parent has lost faith altogether in the sacraments, it is hard for me to see how his own love of Christ—combined with his awareness of his own lack of divinity—would not make him extremely eager to see his child immediately taken into the love of Christ which is so superior to his. If the mother and father have any self-knowledge at all, they will be aware of how much their child is liable to become the victim of their own shortcomings. Even if his parents be the most loving in the world, by comparison with the promise of divine life in eternity, every child's life—

fated as it is to share in the suffering lot of humanity—is a bit like that of Cinderella.

Just as the fear that he will not be loving enough gives to a father the impetus to come closer to Christ for the sake of his child, so, too, he will hope that the infant will grow in the knowledge that God is the true Father, and that his destiny in infinitely greater than that which would flow from the fact of being a child even of parents very rich in money, land, talents, or virtue. We all know of parents who consider themselves not as grateful <u>trustees</u> of a precious being, but rather as <u>possessors</u> of their children. One need not be a student of psychology to be aware of the sufferings which result from such an attitude.

In light of the above, we can see that, far from being something unfree which binds the child, baptism is, in fact, a pledge of his eventual liberty and the seal of his destiny as a beloved child of God.

Holy Communion

> "Take, eat; this is My Body," And He took a cup, and when He had given thanks He gave it to them saying, "Drink of it ... for this is my blood of the

covenant which is poured out for many for the forgiveness of sins!" (Matthew 26:26-28)

Many say that Christ is to be found primarily in loving one's neighbor. They consider misspent the time taken to adore Christ in the Eucharist. To them, taking Communion is less an immediate union with Christ than a symbol of Christ's desire to see his people gathered together at a communal meal.

True as it is that Christ wishes us to find him in the midst of human love, as shall be discussed more in detail in later sections, it is very clear that the truth of Christ's real presence in the Eucharist aims at a still more direct form of love.

Even in human love, we find a great desire actually to be in the <u>presence</u> of the beloved one. If someone would be willing to do anything for another but would shun her presence, she would feel hurt and unloved. Being in the actual presence of someone she loves causes a deep happiness, as his tenderness heals the deep wounds of loneliness. Ultimately, when the love is strong enough, she longs for this person not only to be near her but to become a part of her—in the intimate unity of marriage.

God's Love is Intimate

It appears from the Gospels that Christ wanted very much for us to experience his presence, to have us near him. He would gather his people as a "hen gathers its chicks." (Luke 13:34) He lets the little children come unto him. He suffers the crowds to cluster around him. He asks Peter if he loves him. He even begs his friends to be present in his agony.

The deepest physical desire of lovers is actually to become one with each other, the physical act of intimacy being not only an ecstatic experience in itself but also—where it is the fruit of true love in marriage—a real union of hearts and spirits. This attempt carries within itself something paradoxical—because it is impossible to become totally one with another person under the temporal conditions of individuality. Each one is doomed to return to his own inwardness. Yet, from this experience of union, each takes back a more intimate sense of the unique flavor of the loved one's presence: She is truly a part of him and he, of her. And they live out of this unity of I and Thou, no longer as lone individuals. The truth of this is clearly to be experienced in the negative; for if the bond of love is broken, he becomes alone in quite a new way than before. Without the real presence of the love of his wife, a part of him is dead—the part which came alive in union with her. Thus, by analogy, one often finds in those who have lost their faith in Christ and broken communion with him in the Church that sorrowful quality of a lost soul which can no longer find peace anywhere.

It should not be surprising that Christ in his infinite divine love for men would find a way to come into them, and that this unity is accomplished by an act at once spiritual and physical.

He sees his beloved creatures wandering around aimlessly, yet inwardly locked up in their lonely egoism. Filled with compassion, he longs to enter into them, to comfort them, to let the leaven of his love lift up their spirits. Like a human lover, he cannot bear to see the one he loves bowed down with melancholy, but instead would give anything to be able to inject his own joy into her heart.

Just as one kiss does not suffice a lover, but he would come close to his loved one every day, so Christ offers himself to us in the intimacy of communion every day, if we will. Each day we could live out of the unity of love, fed by the food of divine love, by the very being of Christ our Lover, who wants us to be part of him and, what is just as astounding, wants to be part of us.

Saints and mystics have experienced the truth of the real presence of Christ in the Eucharist in ecstasies not given to most Catholics. Frequently utilizing the analogy of romantic love, they have painted a vivid portrait of how Christ, like an unrequited lover, burns for the day when his beloved (each of us) will open to him so that he can pour his love into that soul, possess it, and, finally, bring it to perfect union with him in eternal bliss.

For most of us, it is not a direct mystical experience to receive communion, but rather an experience in faith. It is necessary to emphasize, however, that faith is an experience. It is not simply a blind decision to believe the incredible; it is a response to something not fully visible but still intimated. There are occasional valid moments in which a very vivid disclosure of this mystery is given, sometimes in the form of a strange longing for Communion, or a deep sense of loss when deprived of receiving, or a feeling of great peace after receiving.

As we become more and more opened by his love, the moments may become more frequent when the waters of that inner fountain overflow into consciousness. At such times, it seems clear this underground source has been slowly increasing throughout years of Holy Communion received in faith.

It is not always understandable why sometimes in life the real nature of Holy Communion as the real presence of Christ is very clear to us in an experiential way, and sometimes not at all. When reading about saints, it can often appear that it is really the result of our own indifference that we experience so little. Much as we might think that we wish to come closer to Christ, actually we fear being inundated with his presence and prefer to live in our own world. However, it is also true that some of the saints went through years of aridity in which they clung to the sacraments by sheer faith, and the darkness which surrounded them made them think they were sharing some of the lonely agonies of Christ himself.

In any case, it is by the fruits that we know of the reality of this union. Unless the receiver of Christ puts up insuperable barriers, the body and blood of Christ become a true source of divine love, just as Christ promised when he instituted it.

Confirmation

> "The love of God has been poured out in our hearts. Through the Holy Spirit." (Romans 5: 5)

The discussion of Communion may leave the impression that love is to be understood primarily in terms of mystical self-surrender. This is one very important facet of love, but there is another one which should not be overlooked: strength.

What does the young person admire more than strength? Hardly anything. It is his/her inability to find a genuine source of real inner power which leads to drifting into the spirit of ambitious competitiveness, or pursuing amusement in despair of living up to any higher ideal, or succumbing to vanity as a way of building up a self-image through the admiration of others, or, finally, falling into rebellious delinquency which pretends not to fear even jail or death.

Many times, the young person identifies lovingness with weakness; for in the world of competition, he or she will easily feel that kindness is vulnerable. Yet, we read in the Song of Songs that "love is strong as death," and the promise of the Holy Spirit, the

Spirit of love, is that of an outpouring of strengths, of wisdom and fortitude and understanding, etc. Our human love is weak; but divine love is power itself, since it is the very root of being. Confirmation signifies the dwelling of the Spirit of love in the spirit of the young person. He or she will not be alone to face the world but rather infused with strength from God—not the phony strength of worldliness or of brutality, but the strength of that unconquerable faith which filled the saints.

The idea that virtue should spring out of the Holy Spirit may be understood by analogy to human love. We find that when two people fall in love, their personalities frequently change. A person, previously very smart in the sense of worldly shrewdness, through wonder at the reality of love, will become smart in the sense of being gifted with understanding. A hard, ambitious person may become one characterized by fidelity to love and the spirit of sacrifice.

Just as these qualities flow out of the inner experience of human love, so do the gifts of the Holy Spirit flow from the inner bond of love the Spirit brings. Real Christian love is so much stronger than any attempt to become virtuous simply through idealism because the Spirit of love becomes ours in a much more intimate way through the sacraments.

At this point an obvious question comes to mind. If the sacrament of Confirmation is so powerful, why are these qualities so little reflected in Catholic youth? I think that it may be because, by the age of confirmation, many young people have little desire to face the world in the Holy Spirit. The sacrament is a gift which lies unopened as they rush out to explore the more enticingly wrapped gifts offered to them in the worldly market place. They behave something like those people who, in the days when marriages of convenience were in style, had not the faintest desire to live out of the sacrament of love; instead, they used their new position for the sake of private schemes of self-aggrandizement. Some very ardent adult Christians confess that the focus of Confirmation for them at the time was the joy of receiving their first gold wristwatch.

How did this situation come about? Partly at fault are forms of religious education which do not make the Christian life particularly vibrant to the young. As the French writer Leon Bloy, who eventually became one of the most devout Catholics of his time, wrote concerning his own religious instruction:

> It was a pretense which shadowy likenesses of priests, stuffed with formulas, wring like soiled seminary linen over young and uninterested brows ... As no formula chopper had thought of looking into his heart, the poor child had been able to retain none of this ill-baked bread and, like so many others, he had vomited it forth almost at once along the verdant path of his 15th year ... (*Pilgrim of the Absolute*).

Here again, <u>even</u> sacraments seem like empty forms when they are not understood in terms of the longing of man for Christ's love and his way of entering into us to satisfy that need.

Also, very often, the fault lies with parents whose piety is only skin-deep and who are much more concerned about the worldly success of their sons and daughters than about their dedication to a Christian life of love. To such parents, religious observance is merely one means of avoiding any detours on the road to affluence, such as unwanted pregnancies or other delinquencies. Hence, they are not particularly alarmed to find that their children have no deep love of Christ and neighbor, as long as they get good grades in school. But they are terrified if their son's love of Christ would lead him to shun all security in favor of a life of Christian service.

If the idea of the Holy Spirit is still vague to you, think of it in terms of the irrepressible yearning within you to be saved from a life fragmented by so many conflicting desires and fears, ambitions and frustrations. Or think of it as that flame which you detected in some ardent priest or Sister or lay person who conveyed to you something of Christianity which you can never succeed in forgetting.

Penance

> "Declare your sins to one another, and pray for one another, that you may find healings." (James 5:16)

Let us begin by considering the psychology of a couple in love who have looked forward to seeing each other all week, and then when the time comes they have a bad quarrel. They withdraw from each other and brood unhappily. Then they realize that there is very little time left to enjoy each other, and so they do everything they can to make up so that the last half hour, at least, may be spent in each other's arms.

By analogy, a person in sin sensing the approach of the communion with Christ and drawn by the desire for this moment of union tries to work out the hateful rages and despairs in his soul. He goes to the confessional and lets the grace of Christ flush out the polluted water in his heart through which the pure stream of God's love can no longer flow.

It is this sacrament that is perhaps the least understood and most scorned by those outside the Church and often also resented by those within. "If God knows you are sorry why go tell a priest?" one hears over and over again.

This question may be divided into two parts. The first is why sorrow should be expressed in words, and the other is why forgiveness should be a sacrament passing through the mediation of the priest.

Turning to the first question, and using the analogy of human love, we can go more deeply into the logic of the emotions attending contrition and forgiveness. When two people are in love, every sensibility is heightened. A person previously smug and self-satisfied finds himself full of sorrow when he sees how his thoughtless actions have wounded his loved one. He longs to change. He cannot stand the fact that whereas his heart is full of love, the long engrained habits of his character bring him to act in unloving ways. Rather than let the woman he loves think that he doesn't care, or that he will never change, he rushes eagerly to say that he is sorry. He doesn't just <u>feel</u> sorry; he also needs to tell her that he is sorry—to make a definite disavowal of his act. Even this does not satisfy him. He needs to know that she accepts his sorrow and, most of all, that his act did not destroy the bond of love irrevocably. The spoken words, "I forgive you," are the seal of this reunion. For a human being, with all his insecurities, it would never be sufficient merely to feel sorrow and to assume forgiveness. One suffering from guilt cannot merely say, "If she loves me, of course she will forgive me." Part of his sorrow is the recognition that his act may really have destroyed something which only he can build up again. Just as the unloving act was a distinct concrete moment, so the act of reconciliation must be a definite moment.

Furthermore, the one who has been unloving must truly will to be his better self in the future. Otherwise, he would be proclaiming by his misdeed that he really does not care. For example, if a couple is engaged to be married, and the man should become involved in a love affair with another girl, this act truly destroys the inner bond of self-giving to his fiancée. Unless he pledges himself to change, he really has given up the original bond and nullified it from his side.

It is in the context of this analogy that the notion of "mortal sin" can be understood in relationship to love. Just as in a human love there are some acts which are unloving but which do not essentially disturb the deeper bond of unity—such as passing moments of irritation—others attack the very essence of the relationship, so in our love of Christ certain acts are a betrayal of that bond and cannot be sloughed off as nothing.

God's Love is Intimate

Some people find it hard to understand why one should describe the various sins of mankind as offenses against Christ. They seem to think of morality as taking place on one level and religion on a different level. This mentality is similar to the reasoning of the unfaithful husband who regards his infidelities as merely chance escapades on so different a level than his love for his wife that he sees no relationship between the two. In his blindness, such a man does not live his selfhood <u>out of the bond of love</u> with his wife, but rather defines himself as a separate ego, one facet of which is to have a wife and another aspect of which is to enjoy making love to other women.

Now, to draw the analogy, there are many ways of showing how sins are, in fact, inwardly related to the betrayal of the I-Thou relationship to Christ. In sin, we turn away from trust in Christ's love and providence in favor of frantically chasing what we think to be our happiness. For example, when one despairs that God really cares about one's future and will send the needed love, one tends to embrace fleeting pleasures. It is significant in this regard that psychological studies tend to see many antisocial acts as negative substitutes for real love. A person <u>steals things</u>

because no one <u>gives love</u>. Transposing this phenomenon into the religious sphere, we can say that since, in fact, Christ continually offers us love and guarantees our final happiness, it is a rejection of this love when we try to grab it for ourselves in ways contrary to his will. Our greed for an immediate satisfaction which we could procure through our own powers blinds us to his love which offers us true happiness as a gift.

To proceed with the analogy, when human love has been betrayed, it is not enough just to feel contrite. One must also say so, promise to change and then receive the forgiveness of the other. It is interesting to note that most psychologists agree on how dangerous it is to mental health to bottle up guilt, and how unloving a relationship becomes when it lacks openness. Similarly, one who acted contrary to the bond of love with Christ longs to tell him so, and to reaffirm his love and to be forgiven. The contrition should be as loud and concrete as the unloving deed was.

The above should make it clear why sorrow for sin seeks a definite verbal expression. Now we are ready to turn to the second question about why this forgiveness should be a sacrament mediated by a priest.

If in human love forgiveness is followed by the embrace of reconciliation, how is this to be duplicated in relationship to Christ, who is not physically present to us? It must be by virtue of some spiritual presence which is yet concrete enough to serve man's need for the full vivid moment. We cannot show that the sacrament of Penance is the only way that Christ could have accomplished this result, but perhaps analysis may help us to understand it as an invention of love by considering the words Christ said to his disciples, "Whose sins you forgive, they are forgiven." (John 20:22) The priest serves not as a particular man—certainly not as a mere busybody, or even as a psychologist of the spirit—but as the visible representative of Christ's forgiving love. This sacrament concretely applies the redemption Christ enacted for those sins which negate, and even sometimes destroy, the bond of love between the soul and God. The grace (divine love) in the words of absolution and the deed of penance reseal the bond between I and Thou.

Many say that it would be better to simply express trust in Christ's love by saying with the congregation prayers of contrition. They think of private confession as a way of emphasizing guilt and fear. The answer, in terms of the analysis of love we are pursuing, is that Penance as a <u>sacrament</u> is more <u>intimate</u>. It makes Christ's love for us even more concrete and consoling than reflecting on his words in the Gospels, for in the sacrament he pours into our trembling hearts his healing, forgiving grace right out of the wound we have made in him by our sins. As we sin as individuals, so we long to be forgiven as individuals. As our misdeeds have cast Christ's love out of our hearts to be replaced by despairing egocentricity, so not only Christ's words but he himself must return to us.

For how many has the confessional represented the open arms of Christ waiting patiently for the return of the Prodigal Son. We have fled from our true Lover, seeking solace in other more tempting goods, only to find ourselves eating corn husks. Or, like Mary Magdalene, we become aware of Christ's pure love for us, and shedding bitter tears, we realize how we have thrown ourselves away. We fall at the feet of Christ no more to remain outside the embrace of this love in morbid self-analysis and despair. There, through the grace of absolution, we are reunited with that love we sought so futilely to replace by attachment to worldly ambitions, material objects, lusts, dreams of fame, etc.

> Certainty, certainty, heartfelt, joy, peace ...
> Joy, joy, joy, tears of joy.
> I have cut myself off from Him ...
> > the fountain of loving waters.
> I have cut myself off from Him,
> > shunned Him, denied Him, crucified Him.
> Let me never be cut off from Him.

So wrote the great French mathematician and philosopher, Pascal, at the moment of his conversion.

Marriage

> "And the two shall become one. What God has joined together, let no man put asunder" (Mark 10:8-9)

Some say that since marriage consists in the mutual self-giving of a man and a woman, there is no reason to introduce Christ as a "third party," or to submit this love to the formalism of a ceremony.

The assumption here is that human love, when it reaches the point of marriage, is in itself so perfect that to think of an added dimension to be reached through the grace of Christ is superfluous. Furthermore, it is assumed that human love is something so intimate to the two people involved that it should exclude all other persons, including Christ.

Such a mentality is understandable if we consider that for many Catholics human love is the most ecstatic reality in their experience, and God is considered more in the light of a harsh lawgiver from on high than as One who wishes to express his love as Emmanuel (God with us). Just as some domineering old uncle may be invited to the wedding, not because of affection but because of societal propriety, so the last thing the happy couple would desire at the sublime moment of loving self-donation to each other would be the presence of God. They go through the service either to placate their relatives, or out of some vague superstitious fear that to go against the mores of the community would bring bad luck.

However, the fact that marriage is a sacrament presupposes that human love is imperfect, and also that there is no one more intimately involved in the love of two persons than Christ, so that when the couple lets him enter into their I-Thou relationship, it becomes more blessed.

The love between two people about to be married is one of the most beautiful phenomena in human life. It is full of tenderness, self-giving, intimacy, and goodness. If this were not so, how could it have been used by Biblical writers as an analogy to the love of God for man? Nonetheless, even though subjectively these two people feel that their love is perfect, objectively speaking, others can already see in it the seeds of imperfection. The desire for self-donation often leads to a possessive consuming of the other's freedom. Such a love engulfs the other, trying to force him into a mold suited to the psychological needs of the lover and stifling his full development as a person. This is not the place to go into details of all the possible ways in which love can be distorted. Suffice it to say that it is rare that one finds in marital love a source of lifelong happiness, so soon do the weeds produced by each person's faults choke off the possibilities of growth.

For these reasons, it seems incredible that any couple would be so foolish as to exclude divine love from entering into their human love right from the start, and thus increase its fervor by the addition of this infinite dimension and diminish those characteristics in each which are so menacing to fulfillment. It is only because so many have lost faith in Christ's love as manifested in the sacraments that they distrust or disregard this source.

That Christ's love ought to enter into the marriage bond to protect and sustain it is very true. But perhaps the way it has been expressed above may leave the impression that it intrudes itself from the outside. It may even sound as if the Catholic couple who marries in the Church is doing so in the sense of taking out life insurance, as if they would use divine love merely as a means for their own security.

We can come to a deeper view by considering that in the Gospels Christ says, "What God has joined together let no man put asunder." (Mark 10:8-9) This phrase is most often quoted in discussions of divorce, but here in this context, it is the fact that <u>God</u> has joined them together which is crucial.

It is considered by many to be very primitive to think that "marriages are made in heaven," and yet there is a great metaphysical foundation underlying this assertion. It is God who has created each human being to be absolutely unique. The individual personality is the invention of his love, and its development is the fruit of its response to his providential care. In a very real and not merely sentimental sense, it is true to say that we meet each person as walking toward us out of God's hands. He is presented to us by God as his creation, distorted by the human environment and his own faults, but nonetheless containing a splendid inner mystery.

This glory may be hidden from the eyes of most people, but it is revealed to love and in love. Many say that love is blind, which is partially true in relationship to some traits. But it is also possible to say that love alone is able to see—in reference to the unique meaning and value of a person. Now, we say that it is in <u>love</u> and through <u>love</u> that the lover sees, but since God is love, it is therefore, equally meaningful to say that it is somehow in <u>God</u> that people come to love one another—whether they are conscious of it or not. Again, if we say that the light of God's love reveals the lovableness of each one to the other, then we may recall that Christ is called by St. John the Light which came to enlighten us all. (John 1:5) If Jesus Christ, the incarnate Love, was willing to come into the mostly loveless daily reality of human existence 2,000 years ago, how much more is he present in the love-filled world of a couple in love.

God's love is the milieu in which all loveableness is discovered, whether each person knows it or not. Now a sacrament is an <u>interior</u> grace of Christ. In the case of Christian marriage, each person freely accepts. the gift of Christ's absolute and divine love into his own love union. They give themselves to each other not only in human love, but also in the midst of the bond of divine love.

To understand this in more concrete terms, recall the gradations of depth which relationships in general are capable of. With acquaintances, one feels most comfortable talking about surface things in a cafeteria. With real friends, one wishes to share at a deeper level than this; one wants to let them into one's emotional states, one's hopes and fears, and so a more private meeting place is sought. For those who are very religious, it is primarily at the level of the spirit that the sharing takes place in their friendships. They feel most happy when they speak about God, pray together, or are together in a church. But with the person one wants to marry, what one is to share is the very innermost life of the other—the unique point where the deepest sources of his being lie. "They shall become two in one flesh." This statement in the Bible does not refer only to sexual intercourse, but also to the way in which this absolute physical giving manifests the inward unity of being. Now, clearly, the level of the sheer individual being of the other is irrevocably joined to the reality of his dynamic spiritual link to Christ "through whom all things were made." And, therefore, it is not surprising that when a lover of Christ falls in love with one of his creatures that she will feel she is touching the mystery of Christ as it comes to a visible point in the beauty of her beloved. The place where they meet is Christ. Not only does she find Christ in him, but she also finds him in Christ. How? When negative factors in the relationship blind her to his lovableness or when physical separation threatens to draw them apart, it is in her contemplative love of Christ that she will find him again—by seeing him freshly in his fullest reality as existing in Christ and because of Christ's love.

It is true that this description of marital love refers more to its peak moments than to its everyday moment-by-moment existence. Nonetheless, there is surely at least a spark of this type of sentiment in every believing Christian when he falls in love, and certainly such emotions reach their peak at the moment of marriage. The subsequent fate of this spark of mystical love, whether it is to become an ash or a flame, is very much related to the degree of their love and the depth of their inward commitment to Christ. If their marital love achieves only the surface level of small talk, or the psychological level of emotional interaction, then it will have failed to achieve its Christian vocation. This distortion not only exists in the religious dimension, but also in the metaphysical one; for love, by nature, seeks a much deeper level than that attained in most marriages. The sharing of being of which children are the most exquisite fruit is clearly meant by nature to be something more intimate and sublime than is evidenced in the feelings of many couples after a number of years of marriage.

What, then, does the couple seek in the sacrament of marriage? They come to Christ and inwardly say, "Thou through whom we were created, who has made each of us lovable and given us the hearts to discover it, do thou live in the midst of our love. Be thou the bond which unites us, so that no human frailty may destroy it. Let this love, which is now so at home in the mystical depths of our beings, always increase. Thou who art Love make our love bond fruitful—a radiant source of new human beings and of more love in the world. We gladly invite thee into our love because it is thou alone who gave us being and blessed us by bringing us together. Through thy loving care, let our destiny be the fulfillment of this love, so that when we come into eternity it may be hand in hand to meet thee face-to-face."

Although the essence of the sacrament of marriage consists in the spoken vow rather than in other elements of ceremony, true lovers of Christ's real presence in the Eucharist are happy to receive each other out of Christ's hands in the midst of the Mass. They are glad of the presence of the priest, the one out of whose hands the mysteries of the other sacraments are dispensed and in whose presence they find a visible image of Christ's joy as he witnesses to their mutual self donation. They joyfully accept this way in which the Church indicates the solemnity and irrevocability of a pledge so rich and beautiful at the moment, yet later so subject to human infidelity.

Their presence in the Church reminds them that it is in the constant return to Christ's presence in the sacraments that they will be able to live up to the promise of this sublime commitment—since all the sacraments work together to increase supernatural love in their souls. They will feel at the end of the ceremony, "Now we have become mystically one. The unity brought about by our human love has been taken up and perfected by returning to its ultimate roots, divine love itself, from which it must never be separated. Now we turn to one another in full joy, coming to the physical expression of the eternal oneness of our spirits."

Holy Orders

> "Then after fasting and praying laid hands on them and sent them (Acts 13:2-3)

There is only one sacrament of Holy Orders. The various orders below the priesthood are degrees of power at the service of the priesthood. The episcopate is the fullness of the priesthood. We write here of the priesthood in this general sense.

Many people have wondered why the following of Christ involves having a priesthood. If all Christians love Christ and he loves them, why do they need a middleman? To some, the priestly function appears to reduce the mystery of Christ's love to mere formulas and rites. Others even see the priest as a sort of front man for a self-serving bureaucracy which lives off the exploitation of man's religious needs, somewhat as a marriage broker makes his money off the romantic exigencies of his clients.

In what way, then, can Christ's founding of the priesthood be considered an invention of love?

Here, again, let us use the analogy of human love. Although love itself is <u>one</u> feeling, there are many ways of expressing it, each with its own special significance. Among these are friendship love, brother and sister love, parental love, and marital love. Each category has its own theme and cannot simply be substituted for another. A friendship, no matter how deep and strong, does not become thereby a marital love; nor does the love of parents for children make the need for friends superfluous.

Now, by analogy, we can say that genuine Christian life results from a response to Christ's intimate self-giving, transforming love, yet some aspects come particularly to the fore in one way of receiving Christ's love, and others in another way. The manner in which Christ gives himself in the midst of the I-Thou relationship of a married couple is different from the way in which his self-giving is expressed in Baptism or Confirmation. We might say that each sacrament involves a new mode of participation in Christ's love. In Baptism, we receive his love as opening a new supernatural flow of life; in Confirmation, his love becomes strength; in Penance, it is his forgiving love we receive.

What the priesthood as a sacrament involves is a specific participation in the <u>sacrificial</u> love of Christ. A man who feels called to the priesthood comes more and more to adore in Christ that love which overflowed even unto the sacrifice of the Cross. His adoration reaches the peak where he longs to commit himself to this mystery and even identify with it.

Simultaneously, his love for men comes to the point where he realizes that he can help them most, not by giving them his human love exclusively but by involving them even more deeply in their I-Thou relationship to Christ. Ordination consecrates a man to the innermost depth of the mystery of the Cross, out of which all the other sacraments flow. When a priest binds his whole life to the reality of this mystery, Christ takes him into the intimacy of his own sacrificial life—which life Christ would see extended throughout space and time in all the sacraments, but particularly in the sacrifice of the Mass.

It may be remarked parenthetically that just as it is not meaningful to ask whether a person becomes more loving through the grace of Baptism or through that of Confirmation—since divine love is being communicated in both instances but in different ways—so it seems equally beside the point to ask whether it is more loving to be a priest or a married man. Certain ways of living the Christian life confer special experiences of his love. The best Christian will be the one whose receptivity of Christ's self-giving love is the most profound in whatever form it comes to him.

Nonetheless, it is true that as in human love the marital state makes <u>possible</u> a depth of intimacy to which no other relationship can compare, so, too, the privilege of the unity with Christ which the priest experiences is something special in itself.

To approach the main question of why the institution of the sacrament of Holy Orders can be seen as an expression of love instead of an organizational obstruction to it, let us consider still another analogy.

Suppose we think of the sacraments as the raft of grace which carries the Christian to his eternal homeland. The priest is the ferryman who has dedicated his whole life to this trip. To ensure that he will actually row people to the true shore, he must be chosen by Christ himself or through former ferrymen who have been so delegated. Because he loves the divine homeland so much, he derives great joy from giving his life to the task of bringing God's people closer to Christ.

By means of this image, several rather controversial questions may become somewhat more clear. Suppose the ferryman were to spend all his time on shore helping the people to improve their own land. This would be a worthy work, but not that for which he was specifically called. The betterment of the love relationships between human beings in the temporal order is a great and genuine Christian vocation. Primarily, this is the role of the laity, and one to which the priest ought to inspire his people in his sermons; but it does not yet touch the special way in which the Christian is to become part of an I-Thou relationship to Christ himself. Ultimately, all who wish will be together in perfect love through Christ in their eternal homeland; this is the hope which the priest holds out and to which he witnesses in part by giving up certain temporal joys in favor of a life consecrated to eternal love.

There is another problem which the image of the raft may illuminate to some degree. This is the question of what to think of priests who perhaps are not as holy as they should be. It is certainly desirable that our ferryman spend his time, as he rows, talking about the raft and the river of love and the distant shore, that is, preaching the Word, administering the sacraments, and living a life of charity. It is marvelous to see the very face of a priest radiantly reflect his vocation of love, but even when that radiance is not there because of betrayal on his part, what really counts is that he ferries the raft to the other shore. The viability of the raft is Christ's love in the grace of the sacraments; it does not, therefore, depend on the personal greatness of the priest but only on his sacramental acts—when Christ becomes present within the souls of his people, individually and mystically. This reflection should not dim the tragedy which such a state of affairs represents, a tragedy in which every Christian who continues to be sinful also participates. If a child whose mother is constantly irritable nonetheless benefits and is strengthened by the food he receives from her hands, how much more so can the Catholic grow on the strength of a food which is actually divine. We have only to examine the lives of saints who lived in periods of terrible decline of virtue in the priesthood to realize vividly how much the sacraments transcend the qualities of the priests who administer them.

A few brief words about the celibacy of the priesthood are relevant here. That celibacy and priesthood have been combined is not an unchangeable teaching of the Church, but rather a Church law which has been in effect for many centuries. However, it can be seen as extremely fitting that those who live for the inner sacrificial mystery of Christ's love should be marked by a devotion so great that this fills their hearts and renders possible, and even glorious, a life in which marital love is sacrificed. One might say that whereas in the marital vocation one self unites to one other self in an intimate I-Thou relation, the priest, as it were, marries in the person of Christ the source of all unions and, therefore, becomes the one most fit to invite all men into this unity with him. The priest, ordained in the power of the Holy Spirit, becomes the "hyphen" in the I-Thou relationship to Christ of each of the recipients of the sacraments. By virtue of his loving movement toward men, he reflects Christ's longing for their love, and by virtue of his consecration to the invisible Christ, he leads men toward God.

Therefore, we see that the priest is not to be considered as a substitute for Christ or as a spiritual bureaucrat. Neither is he simply a guide who through study and prayer is most familiar with the journey ahead. Rather, he is one who has been given power to draw the "raft" of Christ's divine love in the sacraments right up to us. And he does this by consecrating his own life to the mystery, which consecration is matched by Christ's pledge to give himself through the priest in the graces of ordination. Henceforth, through him Christ's invisible love becomes concrete in the sacraments. The priest does not give us himself or a set of formulas or mere signs and symbols; it is Christ who gives himself to us through the mystical words and acts of the priest.

The Anointing of the Sick

> "All those who had any that were sick brought them to him; and he laid hands on every one of them and he healed them." (Luke 4:40)

This sacrament used to be given exclusively to those in danger of death but now is administered to all those who are seriously ill. Every sickness is an intimation of possible death, and in this time of physical and mental anguish we need especially the sense of Christ's presence with us and his providential love. We need to be reminded that he is one with us in every suffering, and that death is the time when our love finally becomes liberated, taking wings to leave this earth for the arms of the divine Lover.

One of the great differences between merely being liked and being loved is that someone who loves us wants to be with us not only when we are happy but also when we suffer. Liking someone often has to do with the fact that he "turns me on," and generally when that someone is in difficulties his companionship is not too pleasant. Therefore, we are both amazed and moved when we discover that someone is not alienated by our sickness or other misfortune. This is a real sign of love. I once saw a very moving sight in a hospital. A wife sitting on her husband's bed. He had just come out of a serious operation. He was in considerable pain. His illness had changed him from a robust character to a limp, weak creature. His wife sat holding his hand, gazing into his face with utmost compassion. Her love may not have cured him physically, just as the Anointing of the Sick may not always cure the illness, yet in allowing his suffering to permeate her—to take up the whole space of her own soul—she seemed to be pledging that he would not be isolated in his pain. It would not be buried in him alone, but was shared within the I-Thou of their love.

So, too, every suffering exists within the I-and-Thou of the soul and Christ. He wants to be present to the sick especially. He sends his priests to anoint them so that he may be present to them concretely. At death, he would be especially near to those whose whole lives have been spent in his company. Have you ever seen a certain type of old woman who faithfully attends Mass every day? It seems to me that to Christ she is like an old wife is to her husband in whose lined face he can still detect the image of his bride. He is impelled to press on her lips a special kiss at the moment of her departure from the earth. Doesn't Christ draw even nearer to those who will soon come into the very center of the mystery through death? "I am the Resurrection and the Life." (John 11:25) In eternity, she will be adorned with a perfect body, fully expressive of the youthful love which will fill her soul.

Throughout Church history, however, it is not the anointing of the good which is most dramatic; rather, it is the final absolution and reconciliation of those who have spent their lives in flight from love and now tremble at the confrontation with the unfailing love of Christ. Think of how skillfully a man will avoid some young girl he seduced and betrayed. The more he tries to forget, the more guilty he feels. Imagine what it would be like if it turns out that such a man's life depended on this very person's forgiveness. Thus, we can get a vivid image of what it must feel like to be at the verge of death confronting the figure of Christ. At such a moment of fear, what could suffice to convince him that he will be saved? A promise of forgiveness would help, but how much more reassuring if she were actually present to forgive him.

This assurance Christ longed to give to his beloved betrayers. "Forgive them, they know not what they do!" (Luke 23:34) A man or woman whose whole life was one long flight from him can yet be reconciled in love if only his final offer of forgiveness is not spurned, and it is this hope which sends priests out to brave the contempt of hardened sinners, bringing them the offer of Christ's visible reconciling sacrament.

God's Love Transforms

His Love Makes Us True Christians

At this point, the reader may blink his eyes in bewilderment. "All this is no doubt beautiful, but what does it have to do with the Church I know: its medieval dogmas which act as a strait jacket to my mind; it repetitious prayers which bore me to death; its constraining moral laws which give me guilt complexes; its ridiculous insistence that one worship God not in the beauty of nature but in a ritualized Sunday Mass to be attended in an ugly building and so on and on?"

Because these feelings are so real to many people, it is essential to show that all the complaints mentioned above can actually appear in another light when related to love.

As in connection with the sacraments, one can see that in each case Christ has invented a way of making his love more intimate to us. I shall try to show how this self-giving love of Christ, which has become so intimately present, actually achieves the effect of transforming us into a Christian people.

"You shall love the Lord your God with all your heart, with all your soul, and with all your mind" (Mt 22:37). In other words, we are to be really transformed. Let us look at the various aspects of Church life from this angle.

Dogma

The word "dogma" is one of the terms in our language most disliked by the liberal humanist and most denigrated by the religious liberal. These people presume that to hold certain truths about God as fixed forever is to destroy the freedom of the spirit, to substitute rigidity for free-flowing expansion, and to foster narrow piety at the expense of mysticism. Yet the claim here shall be made that it is precisely through dogma that we can love the Lord with our whole mind.

To the believer, the recital of the dogmas is like a sacred poem in which all the great truths of his beloved Lord are proclaimed, set into relief, made to glow forever. In the mouths of the Catholic mystics, words turned dry as dust in old books become songs of delight. We can get a glimpse of this change whenever a certain dogma has come alive for us in a spiritual experience, for then we realize how untrue it is to think of dogma as a set of abstractions.

There are many ways to explain the real significance of formulated doctrine. Clearly, its primary function is the revelation of the supreme truths about God which call for an unreserved consent of faith, and it is this aspect which has naturally been given the most consideration in apologetics. Here, however, dogma will be examined only in terms of the analogy of love.

Every love affair has its truths, consecrated in the words said at the moment of falling in love, in verse, or in love letters. These words are unique to each relationship; and yet they are so similar that classical love songs and poems are able to awaken the same memories in everyone who has ever loved. Words like "I love you," "You are beautiful," "You found me and rescued me from loneliness," however trite, nonetheless become fit vessels into which lovers always pour the emotion which goes beyond words. These words make a poem to which many stanzas can be added but none subtracted, and this in itself is an analogy to dogma.

If this analogy seems a bit far-fetched, think about it in the negative. To refuse to say the words, "I love you," rarely shows a noble respect for the nuances of individual subjectivity, as some claim. On the contrary, it almost always indicates a failure to believe in the realities of love which those words so eloquently express. In the same way, refusal to believe in the divinity of Christ most usually reveals a deep uncertainty about the truth of this dogma and, even more, a tragic lack of faith that God <u>could</u> so love us as to die for us.

To proceed with the analogy, a denial of the words "I love you," or even a slight change in them, is to destroy or weaken the bond of love. It is surely not a mere verbal dispute that is involved if the lover changes the words, "You are beautiful," to the phrase, "Women enchant me." Yet some people actually claim that there is no great difference between saying "Christ is the unique divine Son," and saying, "All humans have the aspiration of the divine in them!" To one who has never loved, one woman might just as well be a mere example of womanhood; in fact, it may seem to such an immature man that to love only one girl is imprisoning, whereas to be free to love many is glorious. Through experience he will find, on the contrary, that the very concentration of the feminine qualities of one unique woman is what liberates the flow of his emotions and causes them to come to a real depth and intensity. Similarly, to one who has never believed in the Incarnation, there is little difference between this dogma and its liberal translation into a statement about man's desire for God. But to one who has loved Christ as the unique manifestation of God, the denial of this truth is a radical destruction of the bond of love. It is in the love of the personality of Christ as uniquely divine that all his general thrust toward the divine loses its amorphous quality and becomes a focused burning flame.

The way in which denial of dogma reaches into the center of love is even greater in the case of divine love than in human love because dogma is the record of the absolute, unchangeable love of God for us. It is the crystallization of all truths of divine love so far revealed to us—burning visions of truth sent by the Holy Spirit to prophets, disciples, evangelists and saints, finally reaching verbal form in the words of the pope and the councils. To deny, for instance, that God created us, or that Christ redeemed us by coming to us in the Incarnation cannot be a merely intellectual conclusion. It is to refuse that love which is revealed to us in these events.

In the light of the above, it becomes easier to see why men throughout the ages have become so disturbed about the denial of dogma and why heresy is proclaimed a tragic loss of faith. If one man loses faith in human love, it is tragic, but if he tries to convince all his friends that love is a sham and thereby deprives them of the greatest bliss that human life offers, then his loss of faith becomes a menace.

Martyrs have died for a dogma not because they are "dogmatic" or fanatical personalities, but because the truth about God's love which the dogma proclaims is too precious to be erased from the consciousness of men. To die in this way is surely no more foolish than to die rather than betray a loved one.

Prayer

If faith in dogma can be described as one way in which the mind can participate in the love of God, prayer may be considered as another way.

Many people question whether prayer is meaningful at all. "If God knows everything, why tell him?" Asking such a question presupposes that the main purpose of prayer is to inform God of something. But prayer is really another form of communication altogether. It is a sort of loving dialogue in which one raises all one's <u>thoughts</u> to God.

To refer to the analogy of romantic love, do the words, "I love you," or "Come to me, I need you," ever become superfluous? What would you think of a boy who, when his girlfriend said, "I love you," or "I need you," would reply, "I already <u>know</u> that, so stop boring me"? It would sound very unloving. Of course, he knows that she needs him, and she knows that he knows, but it is part of the pleasure and security of love to feel free to express one's thoughts and feelings.

If even a human lover knows how much love requires expression in words, how much more God knows this. What is prayer if not a long love dialogue in which the soul lays bare to God all its needs, its delights, its love, and its gratitude.

There are various reasons why what seems obvious in human love seems strange in divine love. One would be that the absence of a visible partner in conversation gives to all prayer a quality of foolishness, unless the viewer believes as deeply as the prayer in the reality of a God who cares. Since the nonbeliever in prayer has great difficulty in trusting that God listens, it becomes even more absurd to him to think that God would be willing to hear about such undivine matters as one's messy set of problems or the repetitious prayers of the liturgy. Yet the same person, when in love, would not consider it below his dignity to enjoy the repeated hymns of praising love which his girlfriend sings to him throughout the day; nor would a girl, at the peak of her love for a boy, feel bored with hearing his thoughts about daily events. She is interested in everything about him and is as eager to help him overcome petty annoyances as to come to his aid in grave difficulties.

This is true not only in romantic love but in all profound relationships. It seems strange that often the same person who devotes himself so passionately to openness in relationship to friends and even acquaintances is yet so blind to the value of total sharing with God. When we love someone, we feel free to say anything, not just what might seem correct, but evidently some think of God more as an object of admiration than of love, and so they speak to him exclusively in set terms which they are sure will be right and only about the most important topics. Or, if this seems artificial to them, they do not speak to him at all. The result is that their souls are full of dark corners into which God's light cannot enter because they never bring these feelings to him in prayer.

With regard to liturgical prayers, there is another reason for distrust. Many have learned these prayers by rote as children, and so they find it almost impossible to imagine that other members of the congregation find the liturgical prayers meaningful. Actually, to those who respond to the beauty of these words, saying them is like singing a favorite love song, the repetition of which only adds to its depth, its rhythm becoming like a heartbeat of love itself. Each time the believer says, "Lord, have mercy," with real ardor, it is like one more wave in the ocean of his relationship to Christ, just as in human love each "I love you" is richer in meaning because it includes more moments of misunderstanding which have been overcome by love.

Even at times when a person goes to church in a state of boredom or distraction, the words of the liturgy have the power of a distant echo which reminds him of those valid moments when he experienced them as full of light and peace. They are as comforting to him as a piece of background music which has once been listened to with passionate intensity. At the moment, even though he is forced to be occupied with mundane affairs, at least the music in the background is beautiful. Just so, we are glad to hear the right responses being given to God in the words of the liturgy. Willingly listening to the eternal truths, we at least do not despairingly suppose that the world of our time-bogged thoughts is the genuine reality. Always we hope to be renewed in our love of the Father by joining in the prayer of Jesus Christ together with all the members of his Mystical Body.

Through consideration of the logic of love we have shown that if God is love then it cannot be foolish to come to him prayerfully in the liturgy with all our thoughts and needs. Still, it is possible that a person may prefer silent to spoken prayer, precisely with reference to a different analogy to human love. There are those moments in love when silence becomes full of meaning—when the emotion is greater than any words. This silent way of love is not at all foreign to the prayer life of the lover of God. The prayer of silence has always been part of Catholic worship, though many are unfamiliar with it. If you try spending 10 minutes a day quietly letting God's love permeate you, you will be participating in a very traditional mode of prayer. It is the dialogue of heart speaking to Heart which takes place in an ineffable manner, transcending thoughts or even visions.

Yet it is rarely a matter of either/or: speech or silence. It is surely not impossible for a person to feel that he relates to God only in silence, but this does not seem to fit the usual laws of human psychology. What human lover, no matter how fond of silence, would forego ever speaking the words, "I love you," which overflow like a waterfall out of the superabundance of the heart? It seems that deep silence most often occurs in a space which had already been opened by the words of love that have been spoken, or, in the case of prayer, have been inwardly or outwardly verbalized. We have all experienced or observed the ambiguous uneasiness of silence when the understanding of mutual love is not clear or sure. So, too, silent prayer naturally follows from the attempts of both man and God to stretch human words to the limits of their possibilities through grace. The silence of love is like that which comes at the end of passionate musical coda, the impact of which is completely different from the void of silence which existed before the music began.

Prayer, clearly, is more than simply informing God about our needs. Yet God does not want us to ask for all things. It appears that he wants to give gifts at our request instead of anonymously. As in human love, it spoils a gift somewhat if we don't know where it comes from, since part of the pleasure is the knowledge that this person's love is behind it. But sometimes we do not get what we pray for, and this greatly bewilders us—even causing anguish when the request seems desperate and necessary. This is hard to understand without a total trust in him and a firm conviction of his love, which helps us grasp the fact that there must be some reason why he did not grant us the wish we are so sure is important. A child may implore his mother not to let the doctor give him that painful, frightening injection, but the mother would not be truly loving if she gave into his pleas.

Many times, one goes to a friend for advice and comes away feeling consoled even though no solution to the problem has been found. The reason is that the loving attention the friend has given is worth more than any concrete answer would be. I think that this is what happens very often when we come to God in prayer. Feeling comforted by his love, we realize that the difficulty we had was not so important, and sometimes the very relaxation of tension that follows also makes it possible to find an intelligent solution.

Perhaps the greatest result of prayer is that by constantly bringing all one's thoughts to God, one makes it possible for him to help situate these thoughts in the context of the vocation of love. If the man who prays is willing to openly tell God all that he feels, then he will soon discover what in his life is good and what is evil. Otherwise, he tends to unconsciously play out his thoughts before his own false ego images, or bring them in fantasy before the judgment seat of other unworthy men. Brought before God, the foolish, mediocre, or harmful thoughts may be more readily rejected, and the good ones may receive the strength of God's affirmation. The more a person thinks within this dialogue of love to God, the more his whole being is transformed.

Have you ever found, as I have, that when your thought or feelings are evil you hide from God so as to cherish them in privacy whereas the moment you turn back (convert) to him, the same thoughts become occasions of deep regret and you desire to strive for patience, kindness, and love to replace them. In this way, through prayer, a person gradually moves from a level of consciousness governed by the hopes and fears of egoism to a new plateau in relationship to God.

Law of Love

It appears to many that there is a contradiction between love and law. The laws which the Church promulgates in moral and religious matters seem contrary to the freedom of the spirit of love. For a young person, this feeling is intensified by an inner psychological struggle. Just at the moment when he would like to give free reign to the desire for new experiences of all kinds, he sees the "stop signs" erected by the Church flashing before his eyes, suggesting to him a bitter choice between guilt or frustration.

I should like to suggest that in fact a certain type of law is called for by the nature of love itself, and therefore acts as an aid to "loving the whole strength." There is much emphasis in the New Testament on the way in which Christ both abrogates the law and fulfills it. The law which he freely changed is the ritual law; the law he fulfills is the law of love which he never contradicts and which includes the Ten Commandments.

Love always aims to be strong enough to last forever. Only bitter experience makes people stop striving for such an eternity of love and settle for something less. A man who has just fallen in love with the woman he expects to marry is overwhelmed by the depth of his own feelings. His gaze is directed at the beauty of his beloved and not particularly at the flaws in his own nature which may destroy this love in the future. Occasionally, he gets a glimpse of the sad possibilities to come. The couple has an argument. Is this a prelude to a rift which could widen more and more? It is at such a moment that a person may develop an avid interest in finding out about the laws of love. He studies the wisdom of philosophers, insights of poets, and empirical observations of psychologists.

Similarly, when a person feels a great flowing moment of love of Christ and his neighbor, it seems as if nothing will change this wonderful state of commitment. But soon afterward, his feelings change, and he tends to return to a less demanding level, accepting many compromises, falling into confusion, and even indifference. Then he becomes disgusted with himself and is likely to become interested in finding a system for keeping love alive. He is now willing to try to learn the laws of love.

To follow through with the analogy to human love, let us consider the law of human love, which binds one to fidelity. How differently this demand will be viewed by a person who understands love and one who does not! To a young man who is very attracted to girls but not yet deeply in love, the idea of restricting himself to one person seems like a diminution of freedom. "Why should some girl whom I happen to go out with more regularly than another try to make me feel guilty when I go out with other girls?" He would not understand her words, "If you loved me, you would see that you ought to be faithful to me." He might think that he did love her more than others, but this fact did not make it wrong to date other girls as well. But at the moment that he really falls in love, everything changes. He would want to be with her as often as possible, and the temptation to turn away from his loved one that might arise from a mere physical attraction to another girl would seem to him unworthy and a betrayal. He himself imposes the law of love and refuses to sanction random feelings, recognizing their lure as the enemy of his real happiness. At that moment, the bond becomes the center of his being, and he no longer sees it as an absurd restriction on the pursuit of life experience. Love and freedom become reconciled, for he has used his freedom to choose one unique, irreplaceable person to whom he responds with his whole heart and strength.

Now let us apply these thoughts to the Church law which forbids a person in mortal sin to receive Holy Communion. The Church—following the revelation of God in the Scriptures, the Councils, and the unchanging moral teachings of Christ—claims that certain sins destroy the bond of love between God and man. In accordance with the law of love, a person indulging in these acts may not approach the intimate union with Christ in any attitude other than a penitent one. To one whose spirituality does not emanate from being a love of Christ but rather springs from previous conformity or fear, the time may come when he questions this list of sins. They may seem arbitrary, imposed from the outside, and contrary to Christ's doctrine of love. "Why should the Church intervene between the soul and God?" he asks. "Who are these hypocrites who imply that Christ loves them more than me, so that they are worthy to approach him, and I am not?"

Underlying this attitude, there is indeed a deep psychological truth. If a person has not found absolute love in Christ, anything that impedes his search for other values is regarded negatively. He may frame this search in terms of a moral necessity of being true to <u>himself</u>. Naturally, in a society riddled with hypocrisy, decadence, and mediocrity (which, too often is also the <u>outer</u> face of the Church), his own inner voice seems to him to be the purest guide.

It is only when he hears the voice of God himself as love, whispering to his soul out of the depths of the Church, that he may find that fidelity to the Church will bring about the greatest fulfillment of all that his deepest self has always sought. Given a profound conversion to Christ in the Church, his attitude toward Church law will correspondingly change. Once he achieves a genuine love of the Eucharist, his greatest desire will be to avoid all temptations and sins which would obstruct his approach to this mystery. He will look to the laws of the Church as rules of love teaching him in the concrete what those things are which would destroy the bond of love. He sees the laws of Christ as a necessary means of rooting out the weeds of his egocentricity, and he is grateful for the knowledge that a certain sin will estrange him from Christ because this will act as a deterrent to those destructive forces within himself which he wants to conquer.

This desire to approach the Eucharist in a spirit of love rather than one of guilty betrayal makes him understand the law of the Church which excludes the unrepentant from Communion. Now he sees it, not as an arbitrary Pharisaical restriction but as the embodiment of a basic law of love: repentance and forgiveness must precede union. He understands from the Gospels and from the institution of Penance as a sacrament that Christ's moral laws are not designed to exclude him as wicked, but rather to lead him to turn away from his sins and to accept the forgiving arms of Christ.

Thus, as an example, Christ teaches us that to hate our neighbor is contrary to the love of God. This seems obvious enough in the abstract, but what about a man whose life has been ruined by the unjust actions of his neighbor? His heart is filled with righteous anger. He makes plans for revenge. So just does his cause appear to be that he is ready to contemplate the most violent acts. At this moment, it does not seem obvious at all to him that the actions he is contemplating are sins. This is because he is not acting out of the bond of love to Christ, but out of his own wounds. It is then that he should remember that the hate in his heart is sinful—that it is the most basic law of love that anyone whose soul is filled with hate cannot be Christ's friend. If he nurses these emotions instead of struggling against them, then he can only come back to Christ's presence through the gate of repentance. He must not come to the Eucharist with the kiss of Judas.

The more holy a person becomes, the more his life exemplifies love, and the more he will shudder at the thought of anything which destroys his love of

God. This follows the pattern of human love in marriage: Couples who have found true happiness in marriage will feel a horror of those things which destroy love, from adultery to petty forms of egoism. Because the knowledge of love is something which progresses with experience, an intelligent person will understand the unlikelihood that all the thoughts of wise men about love will make sense to him right away. Nevertheless, he will extend to a person whose general views have been proven to be correct a certain trusting confidence. If this is a sensible procedure with respect to a purely human guide, how much more so should this trust be extended to the Holy Spirit, the great Counselor. Who can possibly know more about what is capable of transforming a man in the spirit of love than God? St. Paul understood this well:

> When I was a child, I used to talk like a child, think like a child, reason like a child. When I became a man, I put childish ways aside. Now we see indistinctly, as in a mirror; then we shall see face to face. My knowledge is im-

perfect now; then I shall know even as I am known. (1 Cor. 13: 11-12)

The Mass

We often hear it said that the Church is not buildings but people, or someone will say, "Christ is with me all day and all week, not only at an obligatory Sunday Mass."

This reaction to formalism in worship is understandable. Nevertheless, if we believe that the Mass is the sacrifice of Christ and that he is really present there in a unique way, it will be possible to see how things deemed by some to be merely "organizational" in Church life actually can be related essentially to the unfolding of love. (The Mass in itself is an inexhaustible, supernatural mystery. What will be described here is only its concrete nature as related to the structure of love.)

It appears clear from the study of human nature that man seeks a definite space and time in which to order his life. Even in nomadic groups such as the gypsies, there is one definite wagon in the caravan which is the space in which a certain family dwells.

When two people fall in love, they seek a spot to call their own—a patch of grass, a section of the beach, a particular table in a cafeteria, etc. At the same time, they dream of eventually having a permanent home which they will fill with the atmosphere of their own personal encounter, furnishing it with all the things they love in common. The same is true of the love of God. While it is possible for man to worship God on the mountaintop, at the beach, or even on a freeway or a subway, his soul yet seeks a place which is consecrated to God's love, a spot in which this love is the <u>only</u> theme. Thus, men of all cultures build religious dwellings.

Seen in this light, the question "What do you think the Church is—<u>that building</u> over there?" evokes a reply deeper than the questioner had in mind. The answer has to be yes or no. We would have to give the same response to: "Is the family its home?" The atmosphere in which love has been daily practiced is a part of love. While love can survive many a change of place, the absence of any location—as in separation of families for years at a time—is experienced as an extreme hardship. This is also true of the life of a Catholic in a country where churches are forbidden. The absence of a particular place given over to the Lord is not experienced as a liberation of the spirit from the bondage of the concrete, as imagined by those who consider it debasing to express their love of God in a mere church building. On the contrary, the people who must live under such conditions build clandestine chapels where Mass is celebrated at the risk of their very lives.

What can be said about <u>space</u> can also be said about <u>time</u>. Often the same person who takes for granted that he will see his girlfriend regularly every Saturday night seems to find the idea of seeing Christ every Sunday morning or Saturday evening an unbearable restriction on the freedom of his spirit. An odd double standard! To see a particular person every Saturday night becomes a ritual which in no way makes the meeting ridiculous. It would only become foolish if love were no longer present. From this viewpoint, the question, "Why do I have to go to Mass on Sundays?" merely reveals the fact that to the questioner the Mass has become a loveless encounter.

Some argue that they find it difficult to attend Sunday Mass because of the large crowds, the pervasive spirit of conformity, the noisiness of small children, and so on. Although there is a great feeling of joy in being at a Mass which is composed of a small group of intimately related Catholics—as can be experienced by going to a selected daily Mass—it is also true that there is a deep meaning in being part of a congregation where the one thing in common is the Mass itself. For one who truly believes in Christ's Eucharistic presence, it is possible to concentrate on this, instead of vainly judging one's neighbor who at least still loves Christ enough to come to Mass. It seems strange that a person who believes that the meaning of life is to love all men should find it difficult to endure the presence of the people next to him in church. Why he feels this way about his fellow Catholics is hard to say, but if such a person would examine his conscience, he would have to admit that his own attitude does little to contribute to the atmosphere of communal love he finds so absent at the Mass.

This is not to deny the way in which worship is enhanced by fine sermons, beautiful music, the presence of a truly ardent congregation—all of which are a part of liturgical renewal. It is only to suggest that the absence of such elements cannot affect the central mystery of Christ's presence in the Mass and in the Mystical Body of his people, and that each participant is called to respond to this according to his own depth of love, independently of what another person in the group might be doing.

All repetitive forms of expression run the risk of becoming automatic, lifeless habits, yet this does not prevent a girl from wanting to end an evening's date with a kiss, or longing to hear certain words repeated over and over again. Even if this action itself has become mere habit, the failure to perform it is sometimes far more significant; it usually reveals a rejection of love. By analogy, to avoid seeking God's presence in church on his chosen day is to refuse to bring to reality the bond of love; it is to turn away from God to the pursuit of a life divorced from his sacramental presence. If going to Mass has become boring to some, it is not usually because of the formal structures, but because Christ in the Mass seems unreal to them. A person who no longer truly believes that Christ is present in the Mass is likely to focus on exterior aspects of Church rites instead of on essentials. His mood is like that of a man who is so disappointed in his blind date that his mind wanders from her to the question of how to spend the least money, or who else in the room might be more interesting.

To proceed with the analogy to human love, but in its positive form, we see that in every loving relationship there are certain moments the memory of which are cherished and often celebrated as anniversaries. So, in a similar way, the liturgy of the Church celebrates the great moments of God's love for man: the birth of Christ; the Crucifixion; the Resurrection; the coming of the Holy Spirit.

Each daily Mass serves to express in its liturgy the basic rhythm of human and divine love. We begin with the acknowledgment of the rift between ourselves and Christ, caused by our turning away from him on the previous day into loveless patterns of behavior: "Lord, have mercy." We remind ourselves of the beauty of God, our great Love: "Glory to God in the Highest." We listen to what he has to say to us: the Readings from Sacred Scripture. We renew our act of faithful commitment to him: the Creed. We offer ourselves to him—not just the attractive part but the whole of our daily lives—and we beg him to renew his redemption of us. Then, Christ takes the lead. We watch in wonder as he again shoulders our sins, renews his sacrifice, reconciles us to each other in peace, gives himself to us in Holy Communion, sealing us to him and to each other through the mystical participation in his body and blood. Transformed by Christ and filled with his strength, we go forth to bring him to the world in which we live.

"Then will I go in to the altar of God, the God of my gladness and joy; then will I give you thanks upon the harp, O God, my God! Why are you so downcast, O my soul? Why do you sigh within me? Hope in God! For I shall again be thanking him, in the presence of my Savior and my God." (Ps. 43: 4-5)

Love of Neighbor

> "You shall love the Lord your God with all your heart...and your neighbor as yourself." (Lk. 10:27)

The idea that a Christian should love all men, seek justice for the oppressed, help the poor, and so on, is well understood. If little space is devoted to it here, it is not because it is a secondary theme in Catholic life, but rather because so much has been written about it in recent books.

The aspect of love of neighbor which will be discussed here is that which finds its embodiment in the much disliked phrase, "love in Christ." I have heard it said: "If you can't love me for <u>myself</u>, but only in <u>Christ</u>, save your phony charity for someone else and leave me out of it." No one likes to be "loved" out of duty. Unfortunately, this abuse of the idea of loving your neighbor in Christ has come to replace the true concept.

Again, let us approach the question by a common analogy to human love. When a woman falls in love with a man, she is very eager to find out what he likes, and she is especially interested in the things he may have made. This is perfectly natural, for, as soon as her love penetrates to the center of his personality, she wants to share all his responses—to participate, if possible, in every vibration of his mind and heart. The objects of his love often open up a new world to the woman who loves him. Suppose he is an artist, and she had never understood art. She will soon be drawn into this world as a natural overflow of her love for him. If he works as a volunteer in a program for the poor, once she begins to participate in his life, she will begin to look with more loving eyes at people whom she perhaps previously regarded as worthless.

If we were to ask whether she really loves the things he loves or only <u>thinks</u> she does because she loves him, it would be hard to decide. Probably, it would be a combination of both. She loves, in themselves, what he has made or loves, but had she not seen them through her love for him, she might not have been drawn to them at all.

The parallel should be obvious. Through Christ, we come to see in a new light what he has made and loves. To love <u>in</u> Christ does not mean that we superimpose an exterior love on an interior indifference; rather, it signifies that we begin to see the intrinsic value of something through our love of Christ.

To employ a geometric image: When self is the center of existence, we can arrange the people around us in circles; some are intimate, while others are only casual friends; others in the outermost circle are strangers. We tend to see them in terms of their ability to make us feel happy or to be useful, or as obstacles to us. From this standpoint, the commandment, "Love your neighbor," or "Love all men," seems totally unreal. Even those dearest to us reveal themselves progressively as riddled with so many unlovable features that we sometimes cannot stand to be with them—and these are the ones we love most!

But if we fall in love with Christ, then <u>he</u> becomes our center. We love him with our whole heart and, wanting to share all his experiences, we soon realize that all people are viewed by him with love. He sees their unlovable qualities and knows that they can be converted into lovable ones. Would he have created them if he did not love them? The lover of Christ becomes filled with wonder at this idea: Every person in the world is to God someone unique and worthy of being. So, despite all that people do in their weakness which conceals their true beauty, he struggles in faith to find their lovable qualities. In some cases, he may have an immediate intuition of what is lovable in another person, and his own love will flow spontaneously. But usually, no matter how much he tries, he cannot by himself see them, so he must return to the source of that person's being, Christ, begging him to make manifest what he sees and to give him the love-sight which will replace the blindness caused by many psychological factors. The ways of the world have taught us that to be is to fear, to fear is to hate, and to hate is to strike out. But Christianity tells us that to be is to love, since God, who is the apex of being, is love. So, it is in him that we will learn to love all that he has made and all that he loves.

If such love of neighbor is not evident in most Christians, it is not because they love God to the exclusion of neighbor but because their love of God is still feeble. It is in the lives of the saints that we can see how divine love inspires heroic love of neighbor in a concrete and visible form. This we will treat in the next section.

Sanctity

There is much talk of getting rid of the plaster saints in the Church. Some identify devotion to the saints exclusively with the custom of praying to vaguely outlined semi-idols of medieval times. They think of the saints as fanatics and religious freaks, with no relevance whatsoever to contemporary problems in the real world.

Quite the contrary, anyone who reads the lives of the saints carefully will discover that these people are heroes of love, persons who really did love God with their whole hearts. Therefore, they were able to respond with love to groups of people in their own times whom everyone despised: slaves, lepers, criminals, terminal cancer patients, street urchins, and so on.

Among the striking elements in the lives of the saints are the <u>intensity</u> of their love of Christ, the degree of <u>sacrifice</u> in their lives, their deep exalted mystical <u>joy</u>, and their consequent untiring love of neighbor.

If we were to meet a couple whose love retained the intensity of the honeymoon period for their whole lives, we would be amazed and delighted. We would not consider them to be fanatics. On the other hand, if a woman who said she was in love would decide to love her husband a little, but not too much, we would not praise her for her common sense so much as we would question the depth of her love. What then, would we think of a person whose religious commitment is summed up in the words, "Sure, I'm religious, but not too much!"

When we consider the life of St. Francis of Assisi, to whom I shall refer frequently because he is probably the saint best known to everyone, it becomes evident that everything he did was characterized by an amazing intensity. He seemed intoxicated with the love of God, of nature, and of people. He was like one who has fallen in love and can think of nothing else but his beloved. Unlike most of us who move from this high state to a gradually lesser degree of fervor, the love of a saint moves upward in a constant crescendo.

This is obviously what Christ desired when he said, "I have come to light a fire on the earth. How I wish the blaze were ignited!" (Luke 12:49) He wanted his love to come into us like a burning flame so that we could radiate light and warmth unceasingly to a world grown dark and cold. It is the intense love of Christ which fired the zeal of all the great missionaries, past and present. They could not contain within themselves the love which filled their spirits. As human love overflows from the embrace of the couple into the children, who have been described as "love made visible," so the missionary's love makes visible new children in Christ.

It is in terms of this intensity of love that the extraordinary sacrifices of the saints can be understood as heroic instead of insane. As the Song of Songs proclaims: "Were one to offer all he owns to purchase love, he would be roundly mocked." We should give all for the pearl of great price, which is Christ. Just as all married couples are called to love each other for their whole lives, no matter what the sacrifices involved, so it is the teaching in the Church that every man is called to become a saint. In the words of Christ:

> You cannot give yourself to God and money.
> Take up your cross and follow me.
> Enter by the narrow gate.
> The lukewarm I will spit out of my mouth.
>
> (Mt.6:24)

For most of us, love, human and divine, is desirable up to the point of suffering and sacrifice. Or, if at first we feel that we would do anything for the person we love, gradually our fervor dies. When we try to pin-point how this happens, I think we would often find that a time came when a sacrifice was demanded of us which we refused to make. This decision is not always made in full consciousness. The moment of the test comes, we let it pass, we forget it; then, one day we discover that our life is not being lived out of intensity of commitment, but has instead become submerged in a variety of disconnected goals with sterile rewards.

Reading the lives of the saints, we are struck by the presence of turning points when these lovers of Christ took up the great challenge. Their love of the good was so great that they staked their lives to win the battle against the evils which surrounded them. As a result of this same "all or nothing" attachment to the good, they were able to overcome in themselves every fault which would make them lazy, inept, betraying servants of Christ. When St. Francis saw a leper coming toward him, he realized that unless he could sacrifice his natural distaste for contact with this repulsive creature, he would be betraying the ideal of love. Who is the leper in our lives from whom we flee?

Some people are able to admire the great deeds of the saints, but still find small asceticisms practiced by some Catholics to be repulsive and even fanatical. To them, it seems rigid and compulsive for a person to try to conform to Christian principles, or very unnatural to eschew trivial vulgar conversations. They think that a person would be dooming himself to failure and self-hatred if he would try to weed out of his heart every movement of lust or anger, even to the point of physically punishing himself.

Here, it may be especially constructive to make a comparison with married love. What causes the change from those early years of tenderness, generosity, and love to these later years of bitter thoughts, sarcastic comments, inner rage, despair, and "quiet desperation"? It is not always some dramatic moment that leads to this tragic transformation. More often, it is a gradual descent in which each small nasty thought or word or feeling is allowed to live freely, instead of being rejected in a spirit of sacrifice for the sake of the triumph of love. If life may be pictured as a battle between the forces of good and evil without and within, what must be the fate of the good side if its soldiers become lazy, sleepy, and so sure of victory that they do not even notice the enemy creeping into their own ranks? So, by analogy, those who imagine that their fervent moments of love for Christ will last forever, and that they will speedily become great apostles of love, mock as fanatical the saints' insistence on watching every thought word and deed. If we wish to love with all the intensity of our being, then we must be ready to sacrifice all things which prevent us from being loving every moment of the day. St. Francis shows us how in the following prayer:

> Lord, make me an instrument of your peace!
> Where there is hatred - let me sow love;
> Where there is injury - pardon;
> Where there is doubt - faith;
> Where there is darkness - light;
> And where there is sadness - joy;
> O Divine Master, grant that I may not so much seek
> To be consoled - as to console;
> To be understood - as to understand;
> To be loved - as to love;
>   for
> It is in giving - that we receive.
> It is in pardoning - that we are pardoned.
> It is in dying - that we are born to eternal life.

The depth of joy which the saint experiences cannot be separated from his conviction of the reality of its source, just as the happiness of a lover disappears when he discovers that the love he imagines to be coming from his beloved is but his own fantasy. The saint's joy comes from the fact that God's love is the apex of being, and to arrive there involves the spirit in something limitless, inexhaustible, and endless. As many writers on mysticism have pointed out, the ecstatic is the true realist because he achieves experiential contact with what,to most of us, is half-hidden and known primarily by faith.

The joyfulness of the saints is not only the result of their having unusually vivid disclosures of God's love. It also comes very much from the fact that they have stripped themselves—by choosing total sacrifice of everything which would prevent Christ from working in their lives. Theirs is the joy of driving at a racing speed in contrast to the jerky pace of those who are trying to go ahead with one foot on the brake!

The saints are the great revolutionaries in this area of loving God and neighbor. Through their total commitment to God, they were able to extend themselves past the boundaries of what their own society is willing to see as lovable. For example, St. Augustine, in his *Confessions*, amazes us with his intimate love of God. Every idea this great philosophic writer had, he related in some way to God—a startling contrast to our normal habit of making compartments which divide reasoning and observation from devotion and spirituality. To St. Francis of Assisi, all of created being is worthy of love. Water and fire and air, thought of by most people as symbolic or useful, he called brother and sister because he loved them so intimately. St. Vincent de Paul discovered the lovableness of slaves and abandoned babies. And different saints through the centuries overcame the lethargy of their fellow citizens by expending enormous energies in the founding of the first free hospitals and schools for the poor.

In more recent times, we have St. Therese of Lisieux, who found ways to turn the most trivial occupations into gifts of love, thus bringing Christ closer to the limited bourgeois class to which she belonged. St. John Bosco, relying solely on daily contributions, was able to feed, clothe, shelter, and train hundreds of street boys in Northern Italy. And a missionary nun, Mother Teresa, worked in the teeming streets of Calcutta, gathering up those dying in rags—to care for and assure them that at least in their last moments of life they are loved and wanted. The list of saints and their deeds of love is endless.

At a time in our society when we tend more and more to view people as statistics, how can the lives of men and women who held that each person is uniquely valuable be considered irrelevant? If we are really interested in the happiness of those closest to us, can we ignore the depth of love which the saints show us is possible through total commitment to Christ? We should want to imitate them, not because of some vainglorious desire to be famous, but because we wish to give ourselves generously to those who need us. But we cannot do this unless we become holy (totally open to Christ); only then, through love, can we give them something of infinite and eternal value.

Catholic veneration of the saints is rooted in this loving reverence which we accord to those who have allowed themselves to be transformed by Christ's love. The saints are the embodiments of grace triumphing over the forces of mediocrity and evil within the spirit of man. As such, they show the possibility of holiness, becoming models to imitate in our lives, and inspirations to light up the darkness which surrounds us all. When we study their lives, we take courage in the knowledge that other human beings succeeded in loving even though they had to face external difficulties and internal obstacles similar to our own. The existence of each saint is a valid moment in the history of salvation.

Because of the radiance of those personalities who love totally, we find them as lovable as people we know personally, and therefore call on their help as participants in Christ's inner life of grace with trusting confidence. By relating to them, we get a foretaste of the final union of all mankind in Christ's Mystical Body. One day, we shall arrive in eternity where we shall dance together in the sheer joy of perfect love.

Each saint makes Christ's loving presence more concrete to us. By analogy, we can say that in their loving response to God they "give birth" to Christ again and again in our midst. Clearly, the human person of whom this can be said, not as a metaphor but as a full reality, is Mary, the Mother of Christ. It is not possible to discuss in any depth or detail what Mary means in Catholic life. Let us only reflect here on the fact that no other human person so aptly fulfills the definition of the self-giving, the intimacy, and the transformation which characterize authentic love. So completely did she prepare herself to receive God's self-giving love that she became the womb in which the Savior himself was born. Her intimate union with Christ makes visible the physical and spiritual inwardness we have said is the hallmark of God's plan for making his love concrete in the sacraments. In her life, given over totally to serving Christ, we find the model of the transformation which is the result of living exclusively in relationship to God.

Mary is the most perfect image of how mankind should respond to God's love. And now that she is so close to Christ in eternity, she is also the image of the maternal aspect of the divine Love. We picture her with open arms receiving into their eternal home all those whom Christ loves. In the words of Goethe describing the entrance of Faust into heaven:

> All things corruptible
> Are but a parable;
> Earth's insufficiency
> Here finds fulfillment;
> Here the ineffable
> Wins life through love;
> Eternal Womanhood
> Leads us above.

Conclusion

If God is love, then ... ? So began this little book. I have tried to show that a God of love could not be a mere object to be admired from a distance, but rather is a self-giving God, who makes more understandable the mystery of the Incarnation and the indwelling of the Holy Spirit within the Church. A God of love also would come to us as intimately as possible, becoming our center in the I-Thou relation instead of being just one exterior factor present to our consciousness—thus making the sacraments part of the logic of love. Because God is love, our relationship to him is not static or purely ritualistic; rather, it transforms us so that we can love God and neighbor with our whole mind, strength and heart—as expressed in the many facets of Catholic doctrine and life.

But such a way of thinking of the Church by no means ends all the difficulties that can be raised. What about the <u>unloving</u> Church, the whole tragic reality of which is recorded not only in the history books, but also in the souls of all those who have turned away from her in anger and disgust? What about us? Do not our daily lives make men wonder how we dare to call ourselves Christian when our behavior is so un-Christlike?

These problems must always agonize us, but they should not discourage us from valiant attempts at inner reform. In the Church, we receive from Christ and the Holy Spirit all the love-energy we need to become saints, and yet we hold out. At times, we may be tempted to ask ourselves: Would it be better not to call ourselves lovers of Christ, since we are so poor at loving? To answer this question affirmatively would be a still further betrayal of the vocation of love. "Lord, to whom shall we go?" bewailed St. Peter. (John 6:68) Even in the moments of greatest despair, we are still aware that it is in Christ's Church that our ultimate salvation lies. Similarly, a married couple—facing a terrible crisis, or after enduring years of frustration and conflict—know that it is not because marriage is evil that they are failing. Rather, they recognize that it is only by returning to the valid moments of their love bond that they will someday be happy again.

Conclusion

The question raised by the fact that so ideal a plan as the Church of love has not been fulfilled in all or even most of its members cannot be answered by abandoning it. No, the answer lies in clinging even more closely to the love of Christ offered in it so as gradually to become part of its renewal.

> "The man without love has known nothing of God, for God is love. God's love was revealed in our midst in this way: he sent his only Son to the world that we might have life through him. Love, then, consists in this: not that we have loved God but that he has loved us and has sent his Son as an offering for our sins ... No one has ever seen God ... He who abides in love abides in God ... Everyone begotten of God conquers the world, and the power that has conquered the world is this faith of ours." (Jn. 4:8-10, 12, 16; Jn 5:4)

But what if I myself have betrayed this love? Perhaps I feel too evil to be in the church. Can Jesus still love me after all I have done?

In human love, the pain of rejection is so great that after many attempts a lover will finally give up. But Christ, after suffering the pain of death at the hands of scornful men, knows that only in divine love can man find happiness. And though we vainly seek fulfillment down every path, he still runs after our fleeing forms like the hound of heaven described in the famous poem of Francis Thompson:

> I fled Him, down the nights and down the days;
> I fled Him, down the arches of the years;
> I fled Him, down the labyrinthine ways
>   Of my own mind; and in the mist of tears
> I hid from Him, and under running laughter.
>   Up vistaed hopes I sped;
>   And shot, precipitated,
> Adown Titanic glooms of chasmed fears,
>   From those strong Feet that
>   followed,
>   followed after.
>   But with unhurrying chase,
>   And unperturbed pace,
> Deliberate speed, majestic instancy,

>   The beat—and a Voice beat
>   More instant than the Feet –
> 'All things betray thee,
>   who betrayest Me.' …
> I said to Dawn: Be sudden—to Eve:
>   Be soon;
>   With thy young skiey blossoms
>   heap me over
>   From this tremendous Lover—
> Float thy vague veil about me,
>   lest He see! …
>   Is my gloom, after all,
> Shade of His hand,
>   outstretched caressingly?
>   'Ah, fondest, blindest, weakest,
>   I am He Whom thou seekest!' …

www.ingramcontent.com/pod-product-compliance
Lightning Source LLC
Chambersburg PA
CBHW060844050426
42453CB00008B/827